Carlos

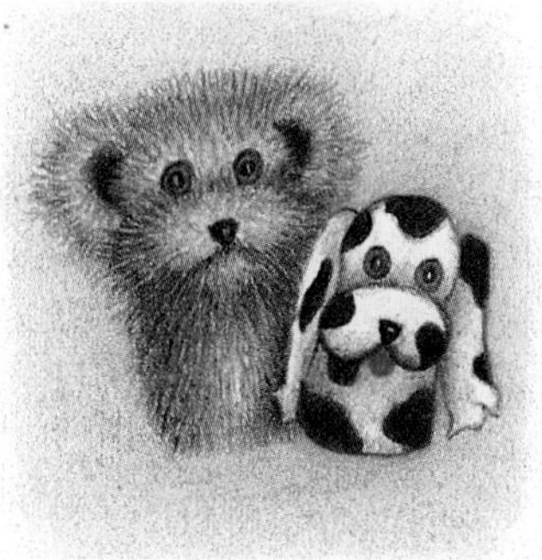

By Judith Womersley

Illustrated by Kate Ellis

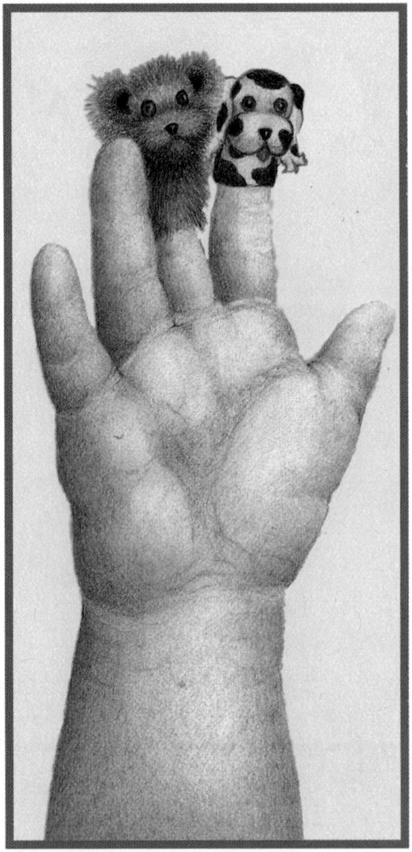

I have five fingers.

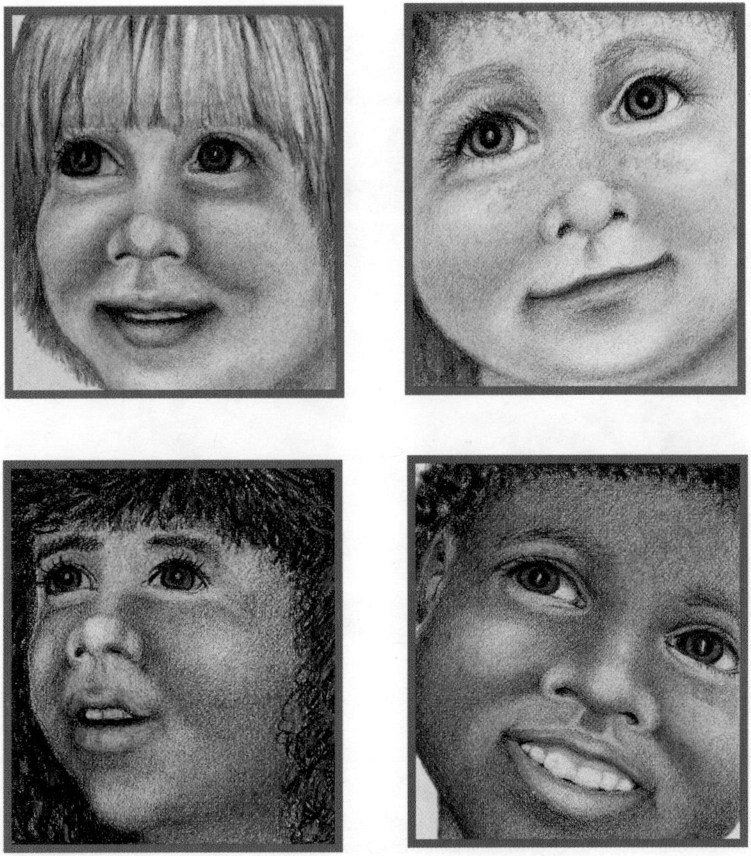

I have four friends.

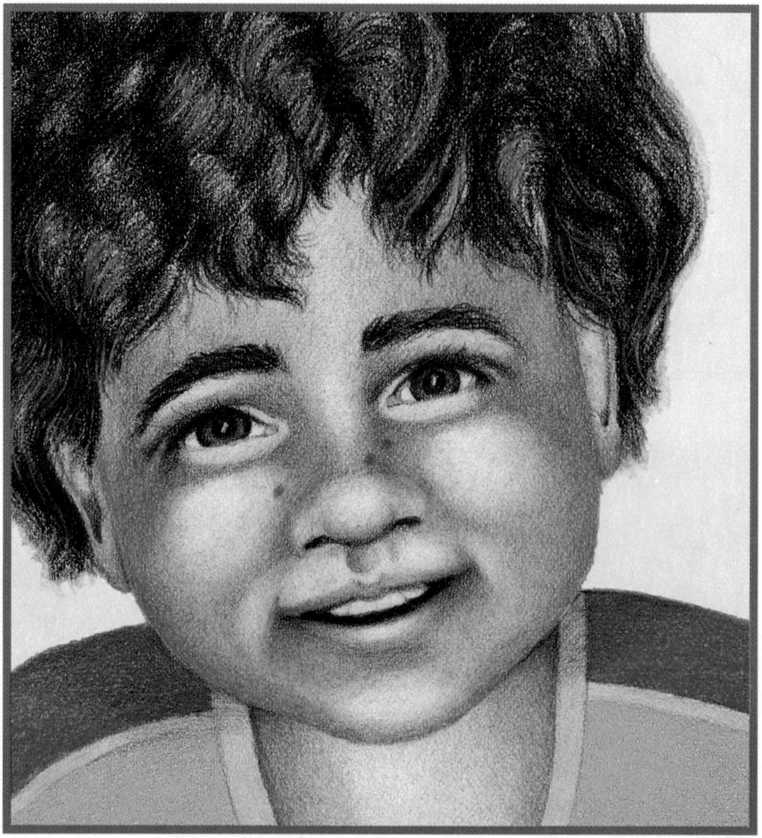

I have three freckles.

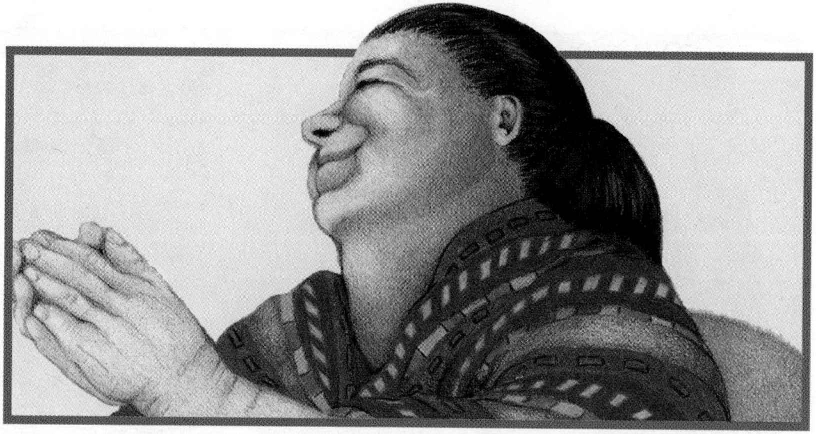

I have two grandmothers.

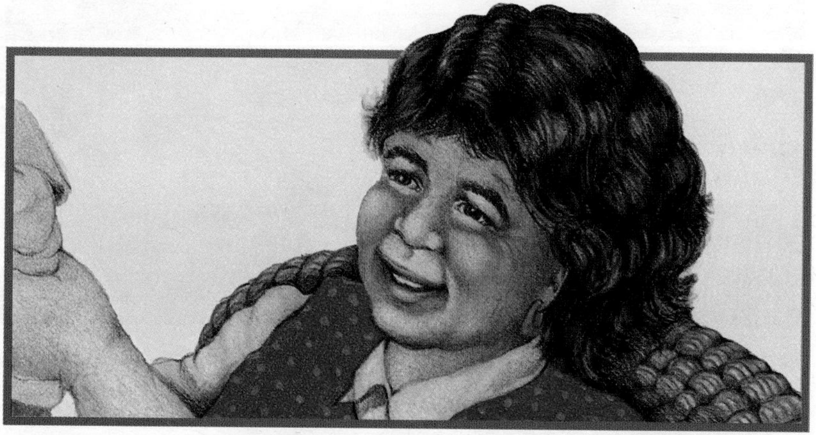

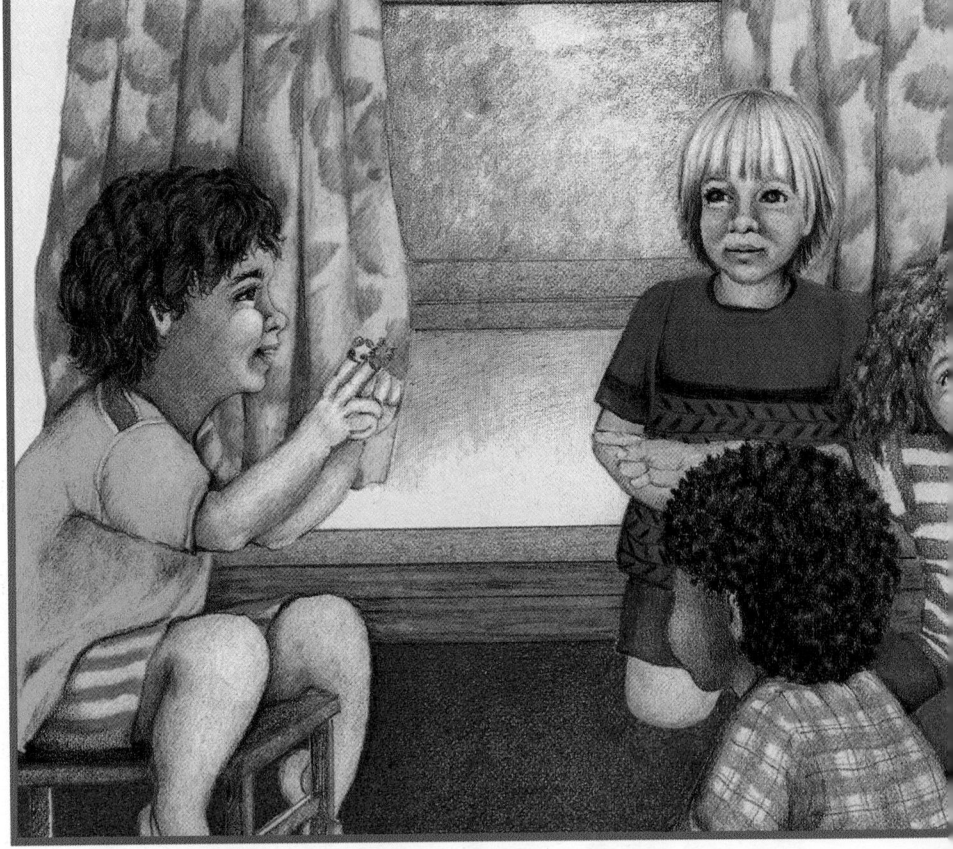

I have one baby sister.

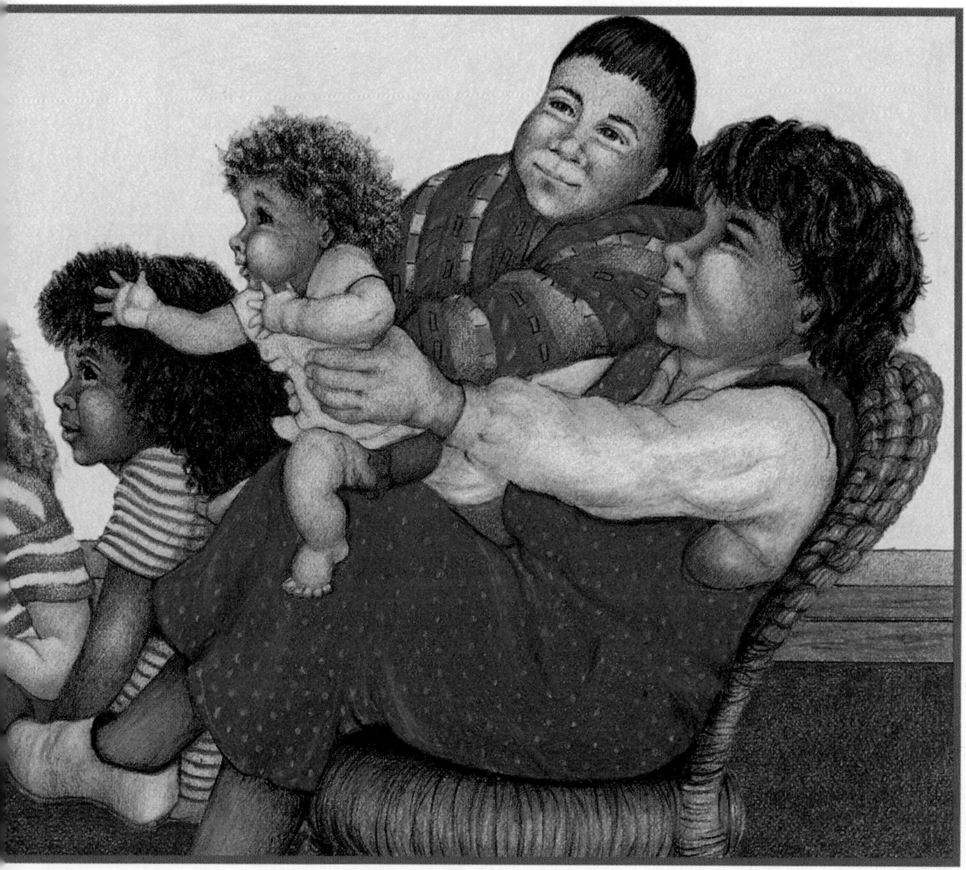

She has . . .

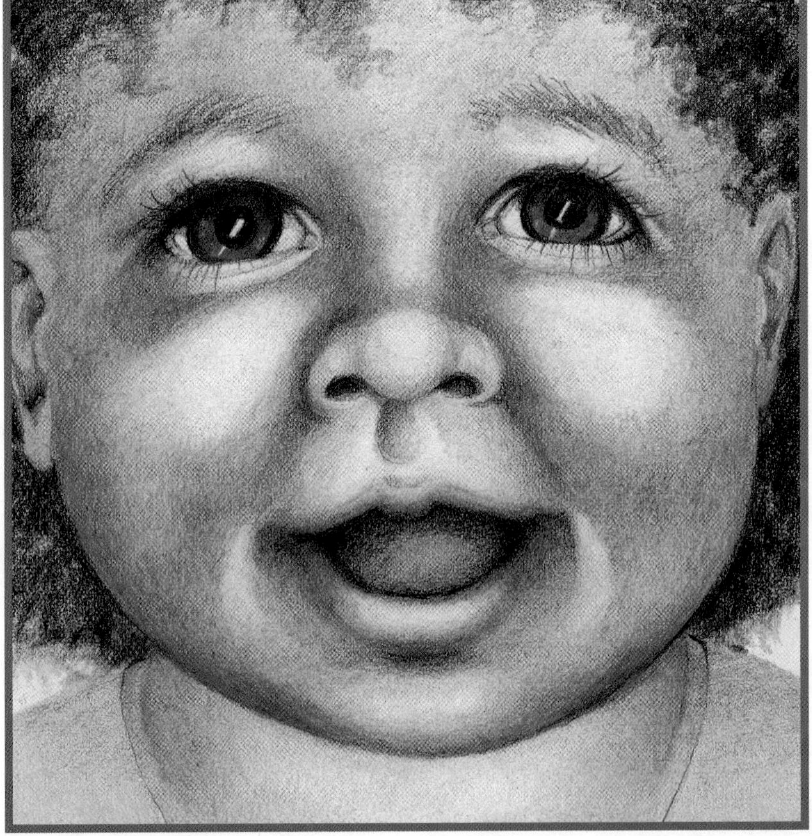

No teeth!